Animal 911
ENVIRONMENTAL THREATS

Animals and Oil Spills

JON BOGART

Gareth Stevens
Publishing

Please visit our website, www.garethstevens.com
For a free color catalog of all our high-quality books,
call toll free 1-800-542-2595 or fax 1-877-542-2596.

Library of Congress Cataloging-in-Publication Data

Bogart, Jon.
Animals and oil spills / by Jon Bogart.
  p. cm. — (Animal 911: environmental threats)
Includes index.
ISBN 978-1-4339-9711-2 (pbk.)
ISBN 978-1-4339-9712-9 (6-pack)
ISBN 978-1-4339-9710-5 (library binding)
1. Oil spills--Environmental aspects—Juvenile literature. 2. Animals—Effect of oil spills on—Juvenile literature. I. Title.
HV4708.B64 2014
636.0832—dc23

First Edition

Published in 2014 by
Gareth Stevens Publishing
111 East 14th Street, Suite 349
New York, NY 10003

© 2014 Gareth Stevens Publishing

Produced by Planman Technologies
Designed by Sandy Kent
Edited by Jon Bogart

Photo credits: Cover : ©National Geographic Image Collection/Alamy/IndiaPicture; Background : LeksusTuss/
Shutterstock.com; Inside: Pg 4: ©National Geographic Image Collection/Alamy/IndiaPicture; Pg 5: Fotokostic/
Shutterstock.com; Pg 6: Jelle vd Wolf/Shutterstock.com; Pg 7: Leonid Ikan/Shutterstock.com; Pg 8: ©US Coast Guard
Photo/Alamy/IndiaPicture; Pg 9: Coast Guard Photo by Petty Officer First Class John Masson; Pg 10: ©ZUMA Wire
Service/Alamy/IndiaPicture; Pg 11: U.S. Coast Guard photo by Petty Officer 3rd Class Robert Brazzell; Pg 12: Universal/
IndiaPicture; Pg 13: ©ZUMA Wire Service/Alamy/IndiaPicture; Pg 14: Universal/IndiaPicture; Pg 15: U.S. COAST GUARD
SLIDE; Pg 16: ©Accent Alaska.com/Alamy/IndiaPicture; Pg 17: ©IDREAMSTOCK/Alamy/IndiaPicture; Pg 18: U.S. COAST
GUARD SLIDE; Pg 19: ©Accent Alaska.com/Alamy/IndiaPicture; Pg 20: ©Nikolai Ignatiev/Alamy/IndiaPicture; Pg 21:
©Gl0ck/Alamy/IndiaPicture; Pg 22: ©Nikolai Ignatiev/Alamy/IndiaPicture; Pg 23: Danny E Hooks/Shutterstock.com; Pg
24: Collection of Doug Helton, NOAA/NOS/ORR; Pg 25: ©Grady Harrison/Alamy/IndiaPicture; Pg 26: Coast Guard Photo
by Petty Officer First Class John Masson; Pg 27: ©Roger Hutchings/Alamy/IndiaPicture; Pg 28: Design Pix/IndiaPicture; Pg
29: Carolyn Cole/Los Angeles Times/USCG.mil; Pg 30: U.S. Coast Guard photo Petty Officer 3rd Class Colin White; Pg 31:
©peter jordan/Alamy/IndiaPicture; Pg 32: ©peter jordan/Alamy/IndiaPicture; Pg 33: Alberto Loyo/Shutterstock.com; Pg
34: Dr. Morley Read/Shutterstock.com; Pg 35: ©joefoxphoto/Alamy/IndiaPicture; Pg 36: ©blickwinkel/Alamy/IndiaPicture;
Pg 37: U.S. Coast Guard photo by Petty Officer 3rd Class Melissa Hauck; Pg 38: U.S. Coast Guard photograph by Petty
Officer 2nd Class Andrew Kendrick; Pg 39: ©paul ridsdale pictures/Alamy/IndiaPicture; Pg 40: Coast Guard photo by Petty
Officer Jonathan R. Cilley; Pg 41: ©Chuck Nacke/Alamy/IndiaPicture; Pg 42: ©Jim McKinley/Alamy/IndiaPicture; Pg 43:
©Accent Alaska.com/Alamy/IndiaPicture; Pg 44: Photoshot/IndiaPicture; Pg 45: U.S. Coast Guard photo by Petty Officer
2nd Class Elizabeth H. Bordelon.

Printed in the United States of America

CPSIA compliance information: Batch #CS13GS. For further information contact Gareth Stevens, New York,
New York at 1-800-542-2595

Contents

Words in the glossary appear in **bold** type the first time they are used in the text.

What Happened to the Water?

On May 20, 2010, a brown pelican glided over the waters of the Gulf of Mexico. The bird was hunting for food. It spotted a fish and dove into the water. The pelican did not catch the fish. Instead it caught a mouthful of gooey, brown **oil**. The pelican tried to get away from the oil by flapping its wings. But it couldn't. Its wings were stuck together. Oil soon covered the bird's entire body.

Why was oil in the water? Where did it come from? Were other birds stuck, too? What about fish? Did the oil affect them as well?

What is Oil?

Oil is actually made of animals—from tiny, one-celled creatures called plankton to huge animals like dinosaurs. After these animals die, they are covered by rock, dirt, and mud. Add heat, pressure, and millions of years, and you get oil!

People use oil for many things. We use it to power our cars, heat our homes and businesses, and make electricity. Oil is important to our lives.

Oil is safe when it is underground or in barrels. But what happens when oil spills?

Gasoline is made from oil, and powers most cars, trucks, and buses. We get gasoline from gas stations like this one.

When Oil Spills, Bad Things Happen

When oil spills, bad things happen to the **environment**. It kills almost everything it touches, including bacteria, insects, and animals. It kills fish and harms the animals that eat fish. Too much contact with oil can cause cancer in animals and humans.

Oil spreads quickly. It only takes 1 quart (0.91 l) of oil to pollute 150,000 gallons (567,811 l) of water!

Effects of Oil Spills on Ecosystems

Spilled oil hurts an **ecosystem**. An ecosystem is a network of plants and animals that depend on one another to live. Think of it as a community of living things. Each living thing in the community is connected to other living things. When one part is poisoned or damaged, the other parts suffer.

Bacteria in water become food for tiny animals like plankton. Fish, snails, and whales eat plankton. Humans eat the fish that ate the plankton. When oil spills occur in water, this entire food chain is damaged.

When oil spills on land, it makes the soil unhealthy. Seeds cannot grow in the poisoned soil, so few new plants grow. When the leaves of plants get coated with oil, sunlight cannot reach the plants. Without sunlight and clean water, plants wither and die. Animals that eat the plants get sick, too. Spilled oil harms the entire ecosystem.

Oil from a leaky pipe covers a lake, polluting the water and poisoning the plants.

Disaster in the Gulf!

British Petroleum (BP) was drilling for oil in the Gulf of Mexico. It used an enormous **oil rig** called the *Deepwater Horizon*. The oil well BP was tapping was 5,000 feet (1,524 m) underwater.

In April 2010, an explosion shook the oil rig. It caused a fire that killed 11 workers. Many other workers were injured. The fire destroyed the giant oil rig. It collapsed and sank into the water.

The explosion caused another disaster. The pipe that carried oil to the surface broke. Millions of gallons of oil poured into the Gulf of Mexico.

Fixing the Leak and Stopping the Spreading Oil

BP had stopped oil leaks before. This leak, however, was different. The broken pipe was about 1 mile (1.6 km) underwater. The company worked day and night trying to fix the broken pipe and stop the flow of oil that was gushing into the gulf. But all their attempts failed. Weeks and then months went by. There seemed to be no way to stop the oil leak.

On the surface of the water, workers tried to contain the oil in large nets called **booms**. They used special ships to skim oil from the water. They also set fires on the oily water. The fires burned the oil, but they also burned birds, fish, and animals.

Workers set fire to a patch of oil in the water. They hoped that burning the oil would remove it from the water.

Death Comes to the Gulf of Mexico

It took BP workers 87 days to stop the oil leak. The *Deepwater Horizon* disaster in the Gulf of Mexico became the largest accidental oil spill ever. The oil covered 572 miles (920 km) of shoreline. It spread across 46,000 square miles (119,139 sq km) of water. About 200 million gallons (757 million l) of oil leaked into the water.

The oil affected everything it touched. It covered fish and killed shrimp. It got inside the feathers of birds and animals. The oil from the oil spill poisoned many marine **habitats**.

Spotlight:
THE BROWN PELICAN

Oil from the oil spill destroyed many pelicans' lives. It got inside their feathers, making the big birds too heavy to fly. In fact, the oil made it hard for them to even float.

Oil in their feathers also made it hard for the pelicans to stay warm. Normally the pelicans' feathers trap air. The air heats the pelicans. But because their feathers were soaked in oil, the pelicans got cold and couldn't warm up.

Workers release a rescued brown pelican.

Death in the Water - Bottlenose Dolphins

Soon after the oil spill, young bottlenose dolphins started washing up on the shore in Louisiana. Some were dead, and many others were seriously ill. The dolphins found it hard to escape from the oil. It got in their eyes. They swallowed it when they opened their mouths to catch fish. The oil coated their skin. It caused cancer in many dolphins.

Another problem facing the dolphins was what to eat. Clean food was hard to find. The oil was killing the fish and shrimp they ate. Some food that wasn't dead had been poisoned.

Death in the Marshes - Kemp's Ridley Sea Turtles

The oil spill was only 50 miles (80 km) from the coast of Louisiana. Tides and wind pushed the oil toward the marshes that line the shore. Marshes are important to a marine ecosystem. Tiny insects, snakes, birds, turtles, spiders, and ducks all live in marshes. By hurting one animal in the marshes, the oil hurt many others.

Kemp's ridley sea turtles live in the marshes. These sea turtles were **endangered** even before the spill. The oil got in the turtles' eyes, throats, and noses. The oil also got into the sand where the turtles laid their eggs and made the baby turtles sick when they hatched. If they made it to the water, it, too, was coated with oil.

This Kemp's ridley sea turtle—and many others like it—were killed by the oil spill.

The Long-Term Impact of the Gulf Oil Spill

Oil spills are hard to clean up and their effects linger for years. Scientists study shrimp in the Gulf of Mexico to get an idea of how the oil spill will affect the environment long-term. As shrimp crawl through the marshes, they eat tiny insects and bits of dead plants. Shrimp help keep the marshes healthy.

Oil from the spill poisoned millions of shrimp. It also hurt much of the life connected to shrimp. Shrimp became sick by eating microscopic organisms that were covered in oil. When bigger animals ate the poisoned shrimp, they became sick. It takes years for this cycle of sickness to stop.

No one knows how long the oil will remain in the gulf water and marshes.

Many dolphins were injured or killed by oil from the *Deepwater Horizon* oil spill.

Disaster in Alaska! The *Exxon Valdez* Oil Spill

It was the middle of the night on March 24, 1989. The *Exxon Valdez* glided out of the Port of Valdez in Alaska. The ship, known as a **supertanker**, was loaded with millions of gallons of Alaskan oil. If all had gone well, the huge ship would have passed through Prince William Sound and moved out into the open sea. But all did not go well.

The supertanker hit an underwater reef. The crash caused 11 million gallons (41.5 million l) of oil to spill into the clear waters of Prince William Sound.

The oil spill was a disaster. The *Exxon Valdez* spill poisoned 10,000 square miles (26,000 sq km) of the sound. It ruined 1,500 miles (2,414 km) of untouched shoreline.

Sea otters, seals, bald eagles, and killer whales live in Prince William Sound. It's home to several national parks and wildlife refuges. The oil spill ruined much of this natural paradise.

No one knows the number of animals killed by the spill. It was impossible to count all the animals that died. But we do know that up to 250,000 seabirds and more than 2,800 sea otters perished. At least 300 harbor seals choked to death on the oil. Over 200 bald eagles and 22 killer whales died. The oil spill also severely harmed the salmon population in Prince William Sound.

Humans suffered as well. Native Americans live off the fish they catch in the water. For a time, native Alaskans were told not to eat the fish they caught in the sound. These and other natural food sources were destroyed or harmed.

Others lost their incomes. More than 30,000 fishermen lost their way of living because they could not fish. Tourists stopped coming to enjoy the wilderness.

Thousands of ducks like this one were killed by the *Exxon Valdez* oil spill.

Oil Spill Cleanup

Because there was no equipment available, cleanup of the *Exxon Valdez* oil spill started slowly. Workers sprayed chemicals on the oil to make it break apart and disperse. Unfortunately, that did not work well.

A big problem for the workers was that the oil had so many places to go. The shoreline of the sound has thousands of coves. It was hard for the workers to get to all these coves to clean the oil off the rocks or to help injured animals.

The *Exxon Valdez* oil spill taught scientists a lesson. They learned that the cleanup itself can hurt the environment it was trying to help!

The Long-Term Impact

Exxon hired 1,100 workers to clean the rocks and beaches. They worked around the clock for months. The workers tried to collect the spilled oil, but they picked up only about 10 percent.

Twenty years after the spill, oil still coats the rocks and stains the sand in parts of Prince William Sound. Many animals continue to suffer from the spill. Some animals have fewer babies. Others are born with birth defects. These are some of the continuing effects of the spill.

Scientists say that it will take up to 30 years for Prince William Sound to recover.

Works set out booms to prevent oil from spreading.

Oil Spill in Russia

Sometimes oil spills on land and not in water. This is what happened near the Kolva River in northern Russia. In 1994, a long pipe used to transport oil started leaking. By the time workers noticed it, 8 months had passed. About 84 million gallons (317 million l) of oil had spilled near the Kolva River.

The spilled oil stayed behind a dike. The dike held because of cold weather. When the weather turned warm, millions of gallons of heavy oil burst through the dike. The oil spread out into streams, marshlands, and muddy bogs. Oil covered 72 square miles (186 sq km) of Russian tundra.

Oil Poisons the Tundra

Tundra is frozen ground. The tundra made it easier for the oil to spread over the land. Although tundra is frozen ground, it is sensitive to disturbance. All living things in the tundra have a shaky hold on life. Trees, mice, ducks, reindeer—they all suffer when anything disturbs the tundra.

The oil spread everywhere. It ran into streams and covered the bases of trees. It covered the only thing that reindeer can eat—**lichen**. About 100,000 reindeer live near the Kolva River, and they depend on lichen to live. Without lichen, reindeer starve. The oil seeped into the river itself and poisoned the salmon, too. Bears that ate the salmon became sick.

Oil from an oil spill turned the white feathers of these geese black.

Kolva River Oil Spill Cleanup

To clean the land, workers pushed the oil into large pits. Then they set fire to it. Burning the oil got rid of it, but it also scarred the land. It takes years before plants begin to grow on those burned places. Burning oil also releases deadly gases into the air. Some birds and animals who breathe this dirty air get sick.

Workers were not able to clean up the Kolva River oil spill completely. Large areas of land are still stained by oil.

1979 – Two Major Oil Spills in One Year

One big oil spill is bad. But what happens when there are two big oil spills in the same year? It's a catastrophe times two!

That's what occurred in 1979. In the same region of the world, two major oil spills sent millions and millions of gallons of oil into the ocean. In this chapter, we read about both of them.

Oil covers a beach after an oil spill. Even with emergency cleanup efforts, it takes many years for beaches to recover.

The Ixtoc I oil spill

The Ixtoc I was a huge oil well. It was 12,000 feet (3,657 m) underwater in the Gulf of Mexico. In June 1979, the well blew apart. All the parts of the system that moved oil out from the ground up to the surface exploded. Oil spilled into the warm waters of the gulf. It took months to cap the oil well and stop the oil spill. By the time the well was capped, almost 4 million gallons (15.1 million l) of oil had spilled into the water.

The oil spread north 160 miles (257 km) to beaches in Texas. Rescue workers found more than 1,200 herons, egrets, and terns covered in oil. Scientists discovered that the oil had made some shrimp grow strange tumors.

The oil spill hurt humans as well. It badly damaged the tourist industry in the region. Big fishing fleets were not allowed to fish and were almost wiped out. Tar balls floated in the water and landed on beaches.

Oil from the Ixtoc I oil spill washed ashore near Brownsville, Texas.

Oil Supertankers Collide in the Caribbean Sea

The second major oil spill happened just one month later. Heavy rain and thick fog hid two supertankers. By the time they saw each other, it was too late. The *Atlantic Empress* and the *Aegean Captain* crashed together. They were just 18 miles (29 km) from the island of Tobago in the Caribbean Sea.

The collision was terrible. Fires erupted on both ships causing the deaths of 27 crewmen. The remaining sailors on the *Atlantic Empress* abandoned ship. Eventually the *Atlantic Empress* sank. All of the 316,363 tons (287 million kg) of oil it was carrying sank with it.

This was one of the worst oil spills ever recorded. How much damage did the oil spill cause in the warm waters of the Caribbean Sea? How much of the dark oil spoiled the beautiful coral reefs? How many sea turtles, reef sharks, and manta rays got sick by swimming in the oil? We will never know. No study of the impact of the oil spill was ever conducted.

Workers tried to rescue the *Atlantic Empress*, but there was nothing they could do. The ship sank, creating an ecological disaster.

Oil Spill in a Lake: The Wabamun Lake Oil Spill

Most of the oil spills we've looked at happened in oceans. This oil spill happened at a beautiful freshwater lake in Alberta, Canada. Wabamun Lake is home to muskrats, migrating birds, wolves, bears, moose, and porcupines. It is famous for northern pike, a fish that can grow to 20 pounds (9 kg).

In August 2005, a freight train that was transporting fuel oil derailed near the lake. No one knows how many gallons of oil spilled into the lake. The train company says only 185,000 gallons (700,301 l) of oil spilled. Others say it was closer to 286,000 gallons (1.08 million l).

For the people and wildlife that live near Wabamun Lake, the number didn't matter. What mattered was that oil was poisoning their beautiful lake.

High winds quickly spread the oil across the lake. Volunteers soon found hundreds of birds and animals soaked in oil. They took all of them to a rescue center. Of the more than 600 birds that were brought in, only 250 or so lived.

The train company did nothing for 4 days. Finally, it announced that oil from the train wreck had spilled into the lake and told people not to drink water from the lake. They were also told not to eat fish caught in the lake. The company advised people to stay away from the oil because it was poisonous.

A worker nets a turtle. In order to survive, it needs to be cleaned of oil.

Cold weather made the cleanup of the oil nearly impossible. The water in the lake had frozen, and the lake was covered in ice by October that year. The cleanup had to wait until the spring of the next year.

Even then, the cleanup was difficult. Wave action moves oil and helps it disperse, but Wabamun Lake is too small to have waves. The oil had time to settle into the shallow waters of the lake. Experts said the effects of the spill would last for up to 5 years.

Other Types of Oil Spills

When we think of oil spills, we often think of accidents. But oil spills happen for many reasons, and they happen in many places.

Sabotage and War - The Persian Gulf Oil Spills

The worst oil spill in history was no accident. In 1991, the Persian Gulf region was involved in a war. The Iraqi army was being driven out of Kuwait. The Iraqis didn't want soldiers to land on the beaches, so they opened the valves on 783 oil wells. They also opened valves on the oil wells in the water. Then they pumped oil out of their oil tankers. All this oil went directly into the waters of the Persian Gulf.

Oil flowed like a river after the oil wells were sabotaged.

The Gulf War oil spill eventually covered 4,000 square miles (10,360 sq km) of water in the Persian Gulf. The oil made its way to the beaches of Saudi Arabia before it moved into the Arabian Sea.

Because of the war, workers had no way to clean up the oil. So the oil traveled freely through the water, where it settled into the 125 miles (201 km) of marshes. The oil poisoned the water in many freshwater wells and ruined them. It also destroyed a thriving crab population.

The oil spill wiped out Kuwait's fishing industry and badly damaged the Saudi shrimp industry. It killed 150,000 shorebirds and up to 250,000 water birds.

It will take decades for these sensitive marshes to fully recover.

Vandalism Causes Trans-Alaska Pipeline Oil Spill

As we have seen, most oil spills are accidental. Sometimes, however, they are deliberate. In 2001, a man shot a hole in the side of the Alaskan oil pipeline. This 800-mile (1,287 km) long pipeline carries oil across the entire state.

Pressure inside the pipeline pushed oil out of the hole. The oil sprayed 75 feet (23 m) out from the hole. In a short time, 285,600 gallons (1,081,113 l) of oil had spilled out. No one saw the man shoot the pipeline. No one knew that oil was poisoning the ground.

The Trans-Alaska oil pipeline is over 800 miles (1,287 km) long. Its route takes it through remote parts of the state.

Oil seeps into marshland. It will take these marshes decades to recover.

This time, however, the environment got lucky. Oil workers flying overhead spotted the oil leak. They called in a pipeline strike team. The team arrived on the scene and shut off the pipeline. They patched the hole in the pipe, and then they started to clean up the oil.

Fortunately there are no rivers and lakes near that section of the pipeline, so no oil found its way into the local water table. Workers could find no evidence that any animals or birds were killed by the oil. This must have been a first—no animals harmed by an oil spill!

Refueling at Sea—West Cork Oil Spill

Some oil tankers carry oil to resupply ships at sea. Sometimes accidents occur when the oil is transferred from one ship to the other.

In 2009, two Russian ships were near the southern coast of Ireland. One ship was resupplying the other with fuel oil. Something happened during the refueling. When the ships left the area, they also left around 100,000 gallons (378,541 l) of oil in the water. The oil slick was just 50 miles (80.5 km) away from the beaches of Ireland.

This aerial view shows a large oil slick in the ocean.

Sea lions rest on an oil-covered beach.

A satellite high above Earth took a picture of the oil slick. The Irish government sent ships to track the slick.

Government officials had reason to worry. The ocean waters near West Cork, Ireland, teem with whales, dolphins, seals, and fish. Officials were afraid that wind and waves would push oil onto the beaches of West Cork.

Fortunately, the wind shifted west and pushed the oil past the southern tip of Ireland into the Atlantic Ocean. No one continued to track the oil. No one knows how many fish it poisoned at sea.

The Russian Navy admitted that its ships spilled the oil. The Russian government paid a large fine to Ireland for the cost of tracking the spill.

Captain's Error: The San Francisco-Oakland Oil Spill

The fog at 4:00 a.m. on November 7, 2007, was too thick to see through. The giant cargo ship *Cosco Busan* was moving through the waters of the San Francisco Bay too quickly. The captain had been taking medicines that made it hard for him to read the charts to guide the ship. By the time a crewman saw the San Francisco-Oakland Bay Bridge, it was too late. The huge ship scraped one of the bridge's huge towers. The collision tore a large gash into the ship's hull. About 60,000 gallons (227,124 l) of fuel spilled into the bay.

A coast guard boat patrols the San Francisco Bay.

Thousands of ducks like these were injured by the San Francisco-Oakland oil spill.

The captain's mistake caused great harm. The oil killed fish eggs and poisoned seals. It covered thousand of birds with oil.

Many people also suffered from the crash. Fishermen could not work. Workers put up signs saying the beaches were closed. Tourists and residents could not enjoy the beaches.

The ship's captain got into trouble. He was found guilty of polluting federal waters. He was fined for harming migratory birds and was sent to federal prison for 10 years.

When Does 25 Equal 3,750,000?

When does 25 equal 3,750,000? This story will explain.

In May 2012, police in New Haven, Connecticut, arrested a man. He had not stolen a car. He had not broken into a store or robbed a bank. His crime? He dumped 25 gallons (94.5 l) of motor oil into a storm drain.

Water flows off gutters, sidewalks, and roads into storm drains. The storm drains flow right into local streams and rivers. This means that the motor oil the man dumped into the drain flowed right into a local river.

If the gasoline in this puddle finds its way into a storm drain, it will poison the habitats of many of the creatures it comes into contact with.

39

Twenty-five gallons may not seem like a lot of oil. But remember what we said at the beginning of the book. One gallon of oil can pollute 150,000 gallons (567,811 l) of water. So how much water did this man pollute? 25 gallons (94.5 l) of oil × 150,000 (567,811 l) = 3,750,000 gallons (53,658,139 l) of polluted water!

The motor oil he dumped didn't just make the fresh water undrinkable. It poisoned fish and their eggs. It got inside the eyes and mouths of river toads. It harmed the ecosystem of that river. And because the water binds all the animals together in a food cycle, when one is poisoned, many get sick.

The police arrested the man because he polluted public water. Polluting water is a crime against the environment.

Oil Spill Cleanup

Workers have learned the best ways to clean up oil after it spills. Here are a few things they have learned:

- **The cleanup method depends on the environment where the spill occurs.** Not all cleanup methods work well for every spill. For example, workers set fire to oil as a way to get rid of it. But sometimes the fires burn endangered animals. The fires set in 2010 after the Deepwater Horizon oil spill burned oil on the surface of the Gulf of Mexico, but they also burned an endangered species–Kemp's ridley sea turtles.

Workers must wear special clothing when cleaning up after an oil spill.

Fire burns a patch of oil contained by an oil boom in the Gulf of Mexico.

- **Be careful! The cleanup can sometimes cause further damage to the environment.** Although workers do not mean to, they often cause more damage to the environment they are trying to clean up. For example, experts have learned that if too much chemical dispersant (used to break up oil) is sprayed on one area of water, it can cause tumors and cancer to grow in wildlife. Another example is from the *Exxon Valdez* oil spill. Scientists discovered that workers damaged the environment by turning over every rock on a beach. The oil by itself was bad. But turning over every rock disturbed the environment even further.

- **Nature and time are the best cleaners.** Experts have learned once the bulk of the oil is cleaned up, nature will repair itself. Many people want to hurry the cleaning process along and make it go quicker. But full restoration of an area damaged by oil takes decades.

Oil Spill Cleanup Techniques

On Water:

- **Booms:** Booms prevent oil from spreading.
- **Burning:** If the oil is fresh, it will burn.
- **Dispersants:** Chemicals that break down the oil into tiny bits are sprayed on the oil.
- **Skimming:** Machines can skim the oil off the top of the water.

On the Beach:

- **Manual treatment:** Workers use shovels and rakes to clean the beach.
- **Mechanical treatment:** Workers use machines to scoop up the oily sand.
- **Hot water and high pressure:** Workers blast hot water at high pressure to clean rocky beaches.
- **Bioremediation:** Fertilizers can break down the oil.
- **Chemical cleaning:** Chemicals such as common dish soap can dissolve some types of oil.

An oil boom helps prevent oil from spreading across this lake.

What can you Do to Help?

Most of us won't be involved in oil spill cleanups. It is dangerous work. Workers need special training. They wear special clothing. So what can you do to help?

- **Oiled Wildlife Care Network:** The Oiled Wildlife Care Network responds to oil spills that affect wildlife. The organization also does research on wildlife rescue and rehabilitation. Donations help them do their work.
- **International Bird Rescue:** The International Bird Rescue organization saves oiled aquatic birds in emergency situations. You can donate to assist them in their efforts.

Conclusion

It takes millions of years for nature to make oil. Oil is safe when it is deep underground. It is safe when it is in barrels or storage tanks. But when oil spills, it poisons almost everything it touches.

As we have seen, oil spilled in nature does tremendous damage. It can hurt an entire ecosystem. It poisons tiny organisms. Then it poisons the animals that feed on those organisms. It ruins the food chain from the smallest animals to the largest. Oil can cause strange tumors and cancer.

We need oil. We use it to produce energy that we depend on in all aspects of our lives. But we need to make sure we don't spill oil. When oil spills, it hurts Earth's creatures.

Workers look for tar balls on a beach in Louisiana.

Glossary

boom: a floating device used to contain oil on a body of water

Deepwater Horizon: name of mobile offshore drilling platform owned by British Petroleum that burned and sank into the Gulf of Mexico in April 2010

ecosystem: a network of plants and animals that depend on one another to live

endangered: species in danger of dying out within 20 years

environment: everything that affects an organism during its lifetime

habitat: the surroundings where an animal or a plant naturally lives

lichen: an organism made of a fungus and an alga that grows on rocks and trees

oil: matter made from the remains of carbon-based organisms under pressure over millions of years

oil rig: a structure used to drill for oil or gas

supertanker: a very large ship used for transporting oil and other liquids

For More Information

Books

deNapoli, Dyan. *The Great Penguin Rescue: 40,000 Penguins, a Devastating Oil Spill, and the Inspiring Story of the World's Largest Animal Rescue*. New York, NY: Free Press, 2011

Person, Stephen. *Saving Animals from Oil Spills*. New York, NY: Bearport Publishing, 2011.

Websites

International Bird Rescue
www.bird-rescue.org
International Bird Rescue exists to save birds affected by oil spills.

Oiled Wildlife Care Network
www.owcn.org/
The Oiled Wildlife Care Network is a response network of more than 30 organizations dedicated to quick, informed response to oil spills that affect animals.

Publisher's note to educators and parents: Our editors have carefully reviewed these websites to ensure that they are suitable for students. Many websites change frequently, however, and we cannot guarantee that a site's future contents will continue to meet our high standards of quality and educational value. Be advised that students should be closely supervised whenever they access the Internet.

Index